Invitation

If you are a dreamer, come in,
If you are a dreamer, a wisher, a liar,
A hope-er, a pray-er, a magic bean buyer...
If you're a pretender, come sit by my fire
For we have some flax-golden tales to spin.
Come in!
Come in!

Shel Silverstein

Little People™ Big Book

About
IMAGINATION

TIME
LIFE for
Children™

ALEXANDRIA, VIRGINIA

Table of Contents

Wishes and Dreams

Giants and Fairies Everywhere

Imagine That!

Merry Mix-ups

Wishes
and
Dreams

If All the World

If all the world
were apple pie,
and all the sea
were ink,
and all the trees
were bread and cheese,
what would we have
to drink?

Mother Goose

Topsy-Turvy Tammy

by Michael J. Pellowski

"opsy-Turvy Tales?" giggled Tammy as she sat down to look at her new book. "What a funny title!" Tammy liked to read all kinds of books. She especially liked silly stories that made her laugh. Sometimes she even imagined herself in the story she was reading.

Tammy took a deep breath and yawned. She felt sleepy, but she wanted to read her Topsy-Turvy book before Mom finished making lunch. "Since this book sounds silly, I'll do something silly, too," said Tammy.

"Instead of starting at the beginning of the book, I'll start at the end." Tammy opened her book to the back page. There she saw a picture of a funny-looking forest. As she began to read, her tired eyes slowly closed.

"BEEP! BEEP! BEEP! Out of the way! Out of the way! You're blocking the road!" a voice hollered.

Tammy's eyes snapped open. She saw she was no longer at home. Where was she? "Did I fall asleep?" she sputtered.

"No! You fell into our book!" the strange voice answered. "And now

6

you are in our way!"

To Tammy's surprise, there was a flock of talking geese standing before her. "Don't geese usually honk?" she mumbled.

"In Topsy-Turvy Land, the geese don't honk. They *BEEP!*" replied the leader of the flock. "Now please move. Winter is coming and it's time for all geese to *walk north!*"

"I thought geese *flew south* for the winter," Tammy said to herself. But she didn't want to argue, so she just moved aside.

"BEEP! BEEP! BEEP!" went the geese as they waddled past. As they vanished into the forest, Tammy heard a great yowling. A frightened dog raced by, chased by a pack of angry cats.

"What kind of place is this?" said Tammy as she leaned back against a tree that had a green trunk and brown leaves.

"It's a magical place," someone answered. Tammy turned to see a polka-dot butterfly perched on a branch above her head. "It's a place where wishes can come true," it said.

"It's very strange here," Tammy sighed. "I wish I could go home."

"You can, but you must first make the right wish," the butterfly replied. "But I can't talk anymore. I have to go! It's time I changed into a caterpillar."

Tammy watched as the butterfly flew away. When it was gone, she started down the path the geese had taken. She hadn't gone far when she saw a fat, pink bear with purple ears riding a bicycle backward. "Look out! Clear a path! Coming through!" yelled the bear as he came toward her.

Tammy jumped out of the way just in time. The bike missed her and crashed into a tall tree.

"Are you all right?" Tammy asked as she ran up to the bear and helped him to his feet. "Why didn't you

watch where you were going?"

"I never watch where I'm going," replied the bear. "I like to watch where I've been."

"What?" called an owl high in the tree the bear had crashed into. "What? What? What?"

"Not *what*, but *who*," corrected Tammy as she stared up at the owl. "You're supposed to say *who*."

"I know *who* is talking," snapped the old owl as he dropped to the ground and started to hop away. "I just wanted to know *what* he said."

"Don't mind the owl," apologized the bear. "He's grumpy because he didn't get a wink of sleep last night, and now he has to work all day."

Tammy shook her head, completely confused, as the bear picked up his bicycle. "I'm going home for lunch now," announced the

bear. "Would you like to join me?"

"Thank you for the invitation," said Tammy politely. "I would love to join you."

"Sorry you decided not to come along," said the bear as he got on his bike.

"But I *do* want to come along," sputtered Tammy. "I'm starved!"

"It's too bad you're not hungry," called the bear as he pedaled off backward. "Bye! Bye!"

· "But I'm *very* hungry," Tammy cried after him. "What's wrong with this awful place?"

"Topsy-Turvy Land isn't an awful place. It's a magical place." Tammy looked up and saw a polka-dot caterpillar crawling by. "It's a place where your wish can come true, if you make your wish in the right way."

"It's a silly place where everything is backward," mumbled Tammy.

Suddenly she realized what she had to do to go home. "Backward!" she shouted. "That's it!" Tammy smiled and shut her eyes. "I wish I could stay in Topsy-Turvy Land forever," she cried. "I *never* want to go home!"

"Wake up, Tammy! You fell asleep reading your book." Slowly Tammy opened her eyes. Her mother was standing before her. Tammy was home at last. "Close your book now," her mother said. "It's time for lunch."

"Yes, Mom," said Tammy. As she shut the book, Tammy looked down at the picture on the back cover. She saw the polka-dot caterpillar smiling up at her. Tammy smiled back at him and then laid *Topsy-Turvy Tales* on the chair. She'd read it after lunch, but next time she would start at the beginning.

LITTLE OR BIG?

You're such a tiny ladybug.
I wish I could be as small as you.
I wonder what it would be like?

Wow! It's like being in a jungle!
The grass is taller than I am!
But maybe I'm too small now.
All my toys are too big to
play with.

14

Maybe it would be more fun to be as big as a mountain. The whole world would look like a doll house!

But then I wouldn't be able to go inside when it rains. I think I'm the right size just the way I am.

15

Giants and Fairies Everywhere

Have You Watched the Fairies?

Have you watched the fairies when the rain is done
Spreading out their little wings to dry them in the sun?
   I have, I have! Isn't it fun?

Have you heard the fairies all among the limes
Singing little fairy tunes to little fairy rhymes?
   I have, I have, lots and lots of times!

Have you seen the fairies dancing in the air,
And dashing off behind the stars to tidy up their hair?
   I have, I have, I've been there!

Rose Fyleman

Me and My Dragon

On days when not
one thing goes right,
I'm glad when it
is finally night.

I sit by the window,
full of gloom,
all by myself
in my dark room.

The window's open
a little bit.
I breathe the air
and stare and sit.

And then I wish
with all my might . . .
until my dragon
comes in sight.

DRAGONS! THERE ARE
NO SUCH THINGS!
Well, maybe not,
but mine has wings.

A huge and wise
and quiet fellow,
his hide is blue,
his eyes are yellow.

My dragon knows
I want a ride.
He's at the window,
right outside.

He reaches in
the room for me.
Outside I go.
We're off! We're free!

23

I hold on tight,
and as I cling
my dragon flaps
each leathery wing.

We whoosh away.
We're in the dark
above the streets,
above the park.

We flap and fly.
Then suddenly
we leave the land.
We're out at sea.

The sky is clear.
There is no storm,
so we head south.
The air grows warm.

A palm tree island
waits below.
It lies in moonlight,
head to toe.

We float above
the shining sand.
Then Dragon shows me
how to land.

His friends, the lizards,
welcome us.
They slap their tails
and make a fuss.

They beat out tunes.
A lizard band!
I dance on Dragon's
giant hand.

A happy, handsome
dancing show.
Then Dragon stops.
It's time to go.

He kneels way down,
and up I climb
to ride upon him
one more time.

The lizards stand
and wave goodbye.
We rise up in
the nighttime sky.

And then I'm home.
Exactly how
I've never known,
I don't know now.

I'm at my window
wondering when
my dragon will
come back again.

What he will do
while we're apart
is wait until
he hears my heart.

Margo Lundell

27

FIND THE ELVES AND FAIRIES

Creeping through the forest glade,
Twinkling in the shadowy shade,
The tiny elves and fairies played.

Can you find:

Fairies having a tea party?
An elf sleeping in the grass?
Fairies racing their dragonflies?
Elves and fairies dancing together?
An elf riding a fish?

*A fairy napping in a
spider-web hammock?*
An elf riding a turtle?
*Young fairies taking ballet
lessons?*

28

Jack and the Beanstalk
A Retelling of a Classic Fairy Tale

Once upon a time, long, long ago, there lived a small boy named Jack. Jack lived with his mother and their cow on a little farm. They were very, very poor and had to work hard for even the smallest crumb of food.

One day, the cow wouldn't give milk.

"You'll have to go to market and sell the cow," said Jack's mother sadly. "Be sure to get a good price. She is all we have left to sell!"

So Jack went to market, leading the cow by the collar.

He had traveled just a short distance when he met a rather funny-looking old man with a long gray beard.

"Do you want to sell that fine-looking cow?"

and sent Jack to bed without dinner.

Early the next morning, Jack peeked out the window and couldn't believe his eyes. Outside was a huge beanstalk, rising into the clouds! Quick as a wink, Jack began to scramble up the stalk. He climbed a long time, and just when he felt he could go no farther, he reached the top.

inquired the old man. "I'll give you five beans for her!"

"What would I do with five old beans?" asked Jack.

"They are magic beans," whispered the old man. "Put them in the ground, and they'll grow to the sky!"

Jack was amazed, so he traded the cow for the beans. He then ran home to tell his mother of his fortune. But when she heard the story, she was so angry that she threw the beans out the window

"My husband doesn't like little children. If he sees you, he'll try to capture you," wheezed the old woman. "But come inside, and I'll give you something to eat. Then you must hide."

Jack had just begun to eat when the whole castle began to shake. He quickly hid behind a chair and peeked out just as a big, ugly giant appeared in the doorway. The giant stomped to the table and sat down. He sniffed the air with his fat nose.

The giant bellowed, *"Do I smell a smelly little boy? I'll catch him, and bounce him, and throw him like a toy!"*

Before him was a stone castle with an old woman standing in the doorway.

"Good morning, ma'am," said Jack politely. "Could you kindly spare a bit of food?"

old woman brought a little brown hen to the table and set her down. "Lay eggs!" bellowed the giant.

The little brown hen began to lay golden eggs, one after another. Soon there was a pile of eggs. Jack watched in amazement, but all the giant did was fall asleep.

"If we had such a hen, Mother wouldn't need to work so hard," thought Jack. He carefully tiptoed over to the table and picked up the little brown hen. Then he ran to the beanstalk and climbed down as fast as he could.

"You smell only your breakfast," said the old woman.

The giant began to eat. He ate two hundred pancakes and ninety eggs, and drank ten gallons of sour milk. While he ate, the

For some time afterward, Jack and his mother would take the hen's eggs to market and use them to buy good food and warm clothes. They lived comfortably until one day when the hen stopped laying. Soon they were as poor as ever. Jack's mother grew sad.

One day, Jack climbed the beanstalk again. He saw the giant's castle and crept inside. On the table were some scraps of food. But just as Jack reached for them, the castle began to shake. The giant appeared in the doorway, his wife behind him.

The giant bellowed, *"Do I smell a smelly little boy? I'll wring him, and swing him, and fling him like a toy!"*

"There's no one here," answered the giant's wife. Jack had hidden himself away. "You smell the dinner I'm making you."

So the giant sat down to dinner. He ate four roast pigs, forty pounds of potatoes, thirty pounds of lima beans, and fifteen gallons of onion juice. While he ate, his wife brought a golden harp to the table and set it down. "Play!" bellowed the giant.

The harp played sweetly. Jack was enchanted by the music, but all the giant did was fall asleep.

"If we had such a harp, Mother would be cheerful," thought Jack. He tiptoed over

34

to the harp, picked it up, and raced for the door. But Jack hadn't gotten very far when the harp began to shriek, "Who are you? Who are you?" at him.

Jack ran as fast as he could for the beanstalk. He quickly climbed down, all the time clutching the golden harp. Suddenly the whole stalk shook violently. The giant had jumped on and was following Jack down the beanstalk!

"Mother! Mother!" cried Jack. "Help! Bring me an ax!"

Jack's mother hurried over with an ax. Jack chopped and chopped until the beanstalk crashed to the ground. And that was the end of the giant!

Jack's mother gently took the little harp into the house. When the harp saw its old friend the hen, it began to play sweetly. The hen heard its music and began to lay golden eggs again. So Jack and his mother never again wanted for anything, and they lived happily ever after.

Imagine That!

If I Had a Cardboard Box

Has anyone a shoe box?
Or any box at all?
I can make houses out of boxes
if they are not too small.

I can put chimneys on them,
and cut out window squares,
and put a smaller box on top
to make a nice upstairs.

The doors have cardboard hinges,
the porch stays up with blocks...
why, I could make a CASTLE
if I had a cardboard box.

Aileen Fisher

AMAZING INVENTIONS

The world is full of amazing inventions. Where are they? All around you! Even the simplest, most ordinary things had to be invented by someone!

Do you see any amazing inventions in this picture? Look at the clues and see if you can guess what they are. On the next page you'll find out more about them.

1.
Can you guess which toy was first made out of a pie plate?

2.
A long time ago, something you wear when you play was worn by gold miners when they worked!

3.
Can you guess what toy was invented to be part of a party costume?

4.
Do you see something that flies high in the sky? It is something we play with. But it was not invented to be a toy. It was used to pass secret codes in China!

5.
Somebody thought up this sweet treat when he ran out of paper dishes.

Anybody can invent something! All it takes is a little imagination.

1.

The toy first made out of a pie plate was the Frisbee, named after the Frisbie Pie Company. In the early 1900's, college students liked to toss empty Frisbie pie plates to each other. The light tin plates floated on air!

2.

Gold miners wore blue jeans in the mid-1800's, during the California Gold Rush. Blue jeans were invented by a young tailor named Levi Strauss. He saw how quickly gold miners wore out their pants. So he made some pants out of stronger material to last a long time. They were an instant hit!

3.

Roller skates were part of a party costume for Joseph Merlin, a Belgian musical instrument maker. Around the mid-1700's, he was invited to a costume party. Joseph wanted to make a big splash at the party, so he made roller skates and rolled into the party, playing the violin. Unfortunately, he didn't know how to stop! He crashed into a mirror and broke his violin. He made a splash, all right.

4.

The high-flying kite was invented thousands of years ago in China. Chinese warriors used kites to send coded messages to each other. The kite's color, shape, pattern, and movements formed the code.

5.

The sweet, tasty ice-cream cone was invented at the St. Louis World's Fair in 1904. At the fair, Arnold Fornachou had an ice-cream stand next to Ernest Hamwi's waffle stand. When Arnold ran out of dishes to serve his ice cream in, he and Ernest put their heads together. They rolled up Ernest's waffles into cones and put Arnold's ice cream on top of them. It was the perfect way to walk and eat ice cream at the same time!

Michael Built a Bicycle

Michael built a bicycle
unsuitable for speed,
it's crammed with more accessories
than anyone could need,
there's an AM-FM radio,
a deck to play cassettes,
a refrigerator-freezer,
and a pair of TV sets.

There are shelves for shirts and sweaters,
there are hangers for his jeans,
a drawer for socks and underwear,
a rack for magazines,
there's a fish tank and a bird cage
perched upon the handlebars,
a bookcase, and a telescope
to watch the moon and stars.

There's a telephone, a blender,
and a stove to cook his meals,
there's a sink to do the dishes
somehow fastened to the wheels,
there's a portable piano,
and a set of model trains,
an automatic bumbershoot
that opens when it rains.

There's a desk for typing letters
on his fabulous machine,
a stall for taking showers,
and a broom to keep things clean,
but you'll never see him ride it,
for it isn't quite complete,
Michael left no room for pedals,
and there isn't any seat.

Jack Prelutsky

43

What Does Anna See?

Anna set up her pad and easel in a meadow one crisp, sunny day. Her friends gathered around her to see what she was painting.

47

Merry
Mix-ups

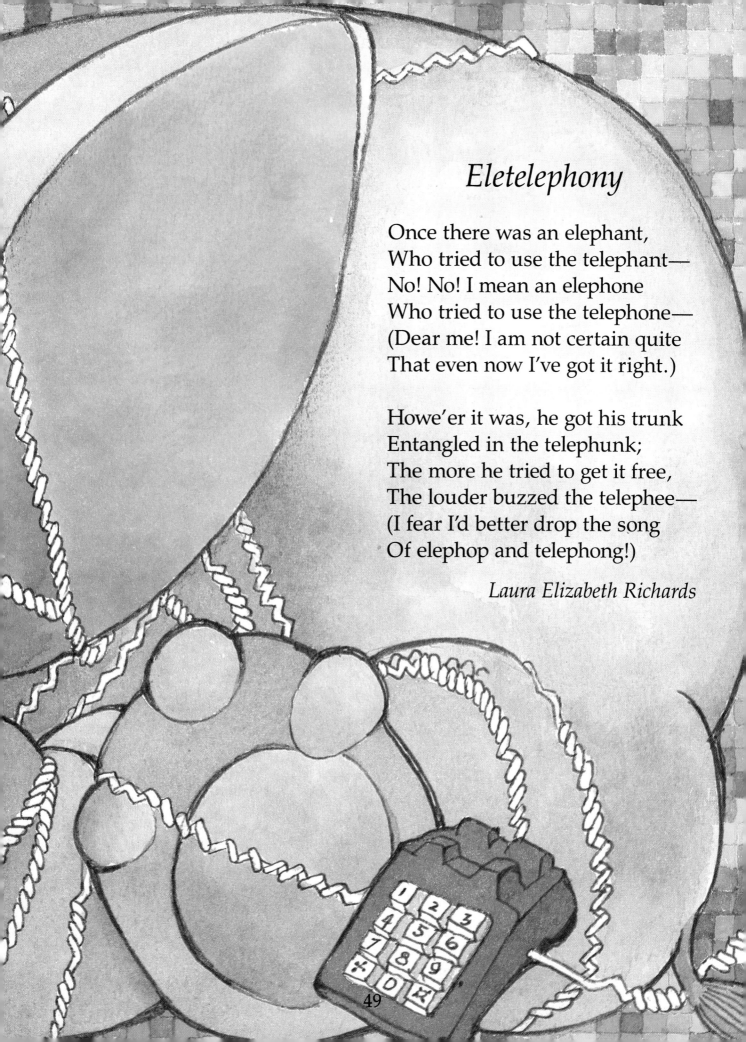

Eletelephony

Once there was an elephant,
Who tried to use the telephant—
No! No! I mean an elephone
Who tried to use the telephone—
(Dear me! I am not certain quite
That even now I've got it right.)

Howe'er it was, he got his trunk
Entangled in the telephunk;
The more he tried to get it free,
The louder buzzed the telephee—
(I fear I'd better drop the song
Of elephop and telephong!)

Laura Elizabeth Richards

49

I Know An Old Lady

I know an old lady who swallowed a  .
I don't know why she swallowed a 🐝 !
I guess she'll die.

I know an old lady who swallowed a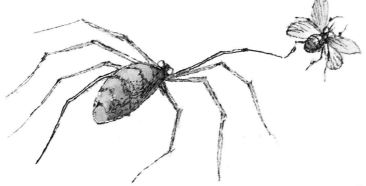
That wiggled and wriggled and tickled inside her.
She swallowed the 🕷 to catch the 🐝,
But I don't know why she swallowed the 🐝!
I guess she'll die.

I know an old lady who swallowed a 🐦.
How absurd, to swallow a 🐦!
She swallowed the 🐦 to catch the 🕷
That wiggled and wriggled and tickled inside her.
She swallowed the 🕷 to catch the 🐝,
But I don't know why she swallowed the 🐝!
I guess she'll die.

I know an old lady who swallowed a .
Imagine that, to swallow a !
She swallowed the  to catch the .
She swallowed the  to catch the
That wiggled and wriggled and tickled inside her.
She swallowed the  to catch the ,
But I don't know why she swallowed the !
I guess she'll die.

I know an old lady who swallowed a .

What a hog, to swallow a !

She swallowed the to catch the .

She swallowed the to catch the .

She swallowed the to catch the .

That wiggled and wriggled and tickled inside her.

She swallowed the to catch the ,

But I don't know why she swallowed the !

I guess she'll die.

I know an old lady who swallowed a .

Just opened her throat and swallowed a !

She swallowed the to catch the .

She swallowed the to catch the .

She swallowed the to catch the .

She swallowed the to catch the

That wiggled and wriggled and tickled inside her.

She swallowed the to catch the ,

But I don't know why she swallowed the !

I guess she'll die.

I know an old lady who swallowed a .
I don't know how she swallowed a !
She swallowed the  to catch the .
She swallowed the  to catch the .
She swallowed the  to catch the .
She swallowed the  to catch the .
She swallowed the  to catch the .
That wiggled and wriggled and tickled inside her.
She swallowed the  to catch the ,
But I don't know why she swallowed the !
I guess she'll die.

I know an old lady who swallowed a .
I don't know why she swallowed the .
She died, of course!

Traditional

Polly's Pets

by *Teddy Slater*

Welcome to Polly's Pretend Pet Shop.
It's filled with the most
fantastic creatures you can imagine.
Come on in and take a look.
There's something here for everyone.

Hungry as a hog and cuddly as a koala bear, the **Livalova** is the perfect pet for finicky eaters. He'll gobble up just about anything on your plate—but leftover liver and soggy spinach are his favorite treats!

If your mom's always complaining about your messy room, imagine what it would be like to have an **Octosniffler** for a pet. She's got the longest nose (just like a hose!) to sniff out the dust balls under your bed. And with all those arms, she can pick up your toys and put them away before you can say "Octosniff!"

And then there's the **Blue-Billed Chimp-Chatterer**, a rare bird indeed. He not only talks, and talks, and talks—he *reads!* And he's never too busy to fly you to the magical, faraway lands in your storybooks.

Kids who hate baths will just love the **Dolphish**. They're as playful as dolphins but not much bigger than goldfish. They like nothing better than frolicking in the tub—and they don't care whether you wash behind your ears or not.

The **Gigglepus** can't talk or walk—and she certainly can't fly. All she can do is chuckle and chortle, titter and twitter, tee-hee, hee-haw, and guffaw! In other words, this funny little furball will keep you laughing from morning to night.

Of course, when it comes to bedtime, there's really nothing better than a plain old dog. He'll give you a big, slurpy good-night kiss and curl up at your feet. . . .

Or maybe you'd rather dream up a super-special pet of your own!

Yellow Butter

Yellow butter purple jelly red jam black bread

Spread it thick
Say it quick

Yellow butter purple jelly red jam black bread

Spread it thicker
Say it quicker

Yellow butter purple jelly red jam black bread

Now repeat it
While you eat it

Yellow butter purple jelly red jam black bread

Don't talk
With your mouth full!

60   Mary Ann Hoberman

A Thought

Think of a whale.
Then
Think of a snail.
Then
Think of a snail on the tail of a whale.
Then
Think of the tail of the whale with no snail.
A whale is so big
And a snail is so small
That there's hardly a difference at all
between
The snail on the tail
And the tail
With no snail.

Mary Ann Hoberman

SNAIL ON TAIL

TAIL WITHOUT SNAIL

Sing Me a Song of Teapots and Trumpets

Sing me a song
of teapots and trumpets:
Trumpots and teapets
And tippets and taps,
trippers and trappers
and jelly bean wrappers
and pigs in pajamas
with zippers and snaps.

Sing me a song
of sneakers and snoopers:
Snookers and sneapers
and snappers and snacks,
snorkels and snarkles,
a seagull that gargles,
and gargoyles and gryphons
and other knickknacks.

62

Sing me a song
of parsnips and pickles:
and pumpkins and pears,
plumbers and mummers
and kettle drum drummers
and plum jam (yum-yum jam)
all over their chairs.

Sing me a song—
but never you mind it!
I've had enough
of this nonsense. Don't cry.
Criers and fliers
and onion ring fryers—
It's more than I want to put up with!
Good-by!

N.M. Bodecker

Little People™ Big Book About IMAGINATION

TIME-LIFE for CHILDREN™

Publisher: Robert H. Smith
Managing Editor: Neil Kagan
Associate Editors: Jean Burke Crawford
  Patricia Daniels
Marketing Director: Ruth P. Stevens
Promotion Director: Kathleen B. Tresnak
Associate Promotion Director: Jane B. Welihozkiy
Production Manager: Prudence G. Harris
Editorial Consultants: Jacqueline A. Ball
  Sara Mark

PRODUCED BY PARACHUTE PRESS, INC.

Editorial Director: Joan Waricha
Editors: Christopher Medina, Jane Stine,
  Wendy Wax
Writers: Margo Lundell, Michael Pellowski,
  Thelma Slater, Natalie Standiford,
  Jean Waricha
Designer: Lillian Lovitt
Illustrators: Yvette Banek, Pat and Robin DeWitt,
  Dennis Hockerman, Pat Merrel,
  Allan Neuwirth, John O'Brian,
  John Speirs, John Wallner,
  Ann Wilson, Tad Zar

Time-Life Books Inc. is a wholly owned subsidiary of THE TIME INC. BOOK COMPANY.

TIME-LIFE is a trademark of Time Warner Inc. U.S.A.

FISHER-PRICE, LITTLE PEOPLE and AWNING DESIGN are trademarks of Fisher-Price, Division of The Quaker Oats Company, and are used under license.

Time-Life Books Inc. offers a wide range of fine publications, including home video products. For subscription information, call 1-800-621-7026 or write TIME-LIFE BOOKS, P.O. Box C-32068, Richmond, Virginia 23261-2068.

ACKNOWLEDGMENTS

Every effort has been made to trace the ownership of all copyrighted material and to secure the necessary permissions to reprint these selections. If any question arises as to the use of any material, the editor and the publisher, while expressing regret for any inadvertent error, will make the necessary correction in future printings.

Grateful acknowledgment is made to the following for permission to reprint copyrighted material: Jonathan Cape, Ltd. for United Kingdom rights for "Invitation" from WHERE THE SIDEWALK ENDS by Shel Silverstein. Copyright © 1974 by Evil Eye Music, Inc. Doubleday, a division of Bantam, Doubleday, Dell Publishing Group, Inc. for "Have You Watched the Fairies" from FAIRIES AND CHIMNEYS by Rose Fyleman. Copyright © 1918, 1920 by George Doran. Aileen Fisher for "If I Had A Cardboard Box." Greenwillow Books (a division of William Morrow & Co.) for "Michael Built A Bicycle" from THE NEW KID ON THE BLOCK by Jack Prelutsky. Copyright © 1984 by Jack Prelutsky. Harper & Row, Publishers, Inc. for "Invitation" from WHERE THE SIDEWALK ENDS by Shel Silverstein. Copyright © 1974 by Evil Eye Music, Inc. Little, Brown and Co. for "Eletelephony" from TIRRA LIRRA: RHYMES OLD AND NEW by Laura E. Richards. Copyright © 1930, 1932 by Laura E. Richards, renewed 1960 by Hamilton Richards. Gina Maccoby Literary Agency for "A Thought" and "Yellow Butter Purple Jelly Red Jam Black Bread" from YELLOW BUTTER PURPLE JELLY RED JAM BLACK BREAD by Mary Ann Hoberman. Copyright © 1981 by Mary Ann Hoberman.

Library of Congress Cataloging in Publication Data

Little people big book about imagination.
    p.   cm.
    Summary: A collection of stories, poems, and essays on the theme of imagination.
    ISBN 0-8094-7479-4.—ISBN 0-8094-7480-8 (lib. bdg.)
    1. Imagination—Literary collections.   [1. Imagination—Literary collections.]
PZ5.L72575   1990
808.8'99282—dc20

89-48162
CIP
AC

TIME-LIFE BOOKS
ALEXANDRIA, VIRGINIA

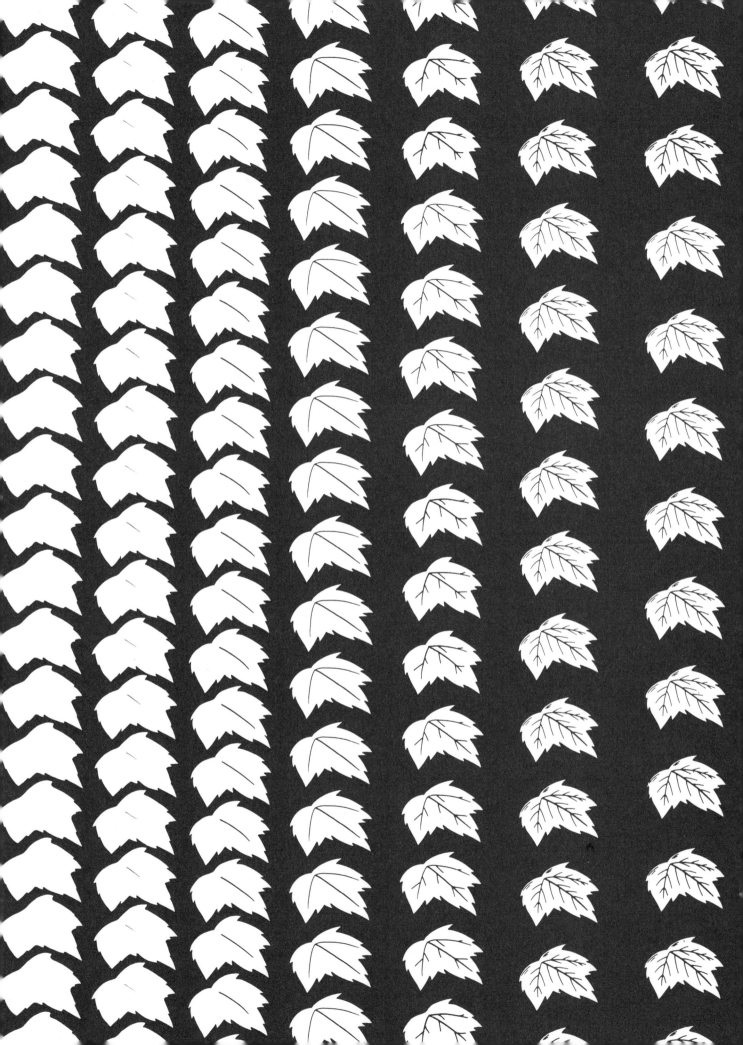

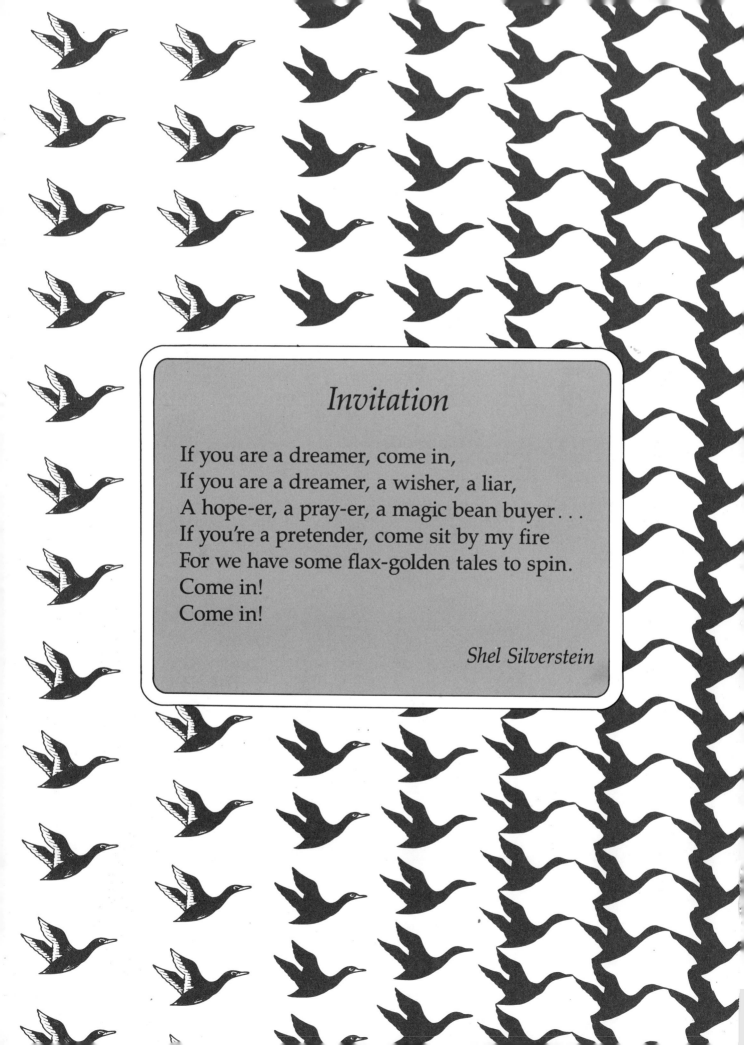

Invitation

If you are a dreamer, come in,
If you are a dreamer, a wisher, a liar,
A hope-er, a pray-er, a magic bean buyer . . .
If you're a pretender, come sit by my fire
For we have some flax-golden tales to spin.
Come in!
Come in!

Shel Silverstein